HISS, SPIT BITE - DEADLY SNAKES

SNAKES FOR KIDS
CHILDREN'S REPTILE & AMPHIBIAN BOOKS

BABY PROFESSOR

EDUCATION KIDS

Speedy Publishing LLC

40 E. Main St. #1156

Newark, DE 19711

www.speedypublishing.com

Copyright 2017

In this book, we're going to talk about deadly snakes around the world. So, let's get right to it!

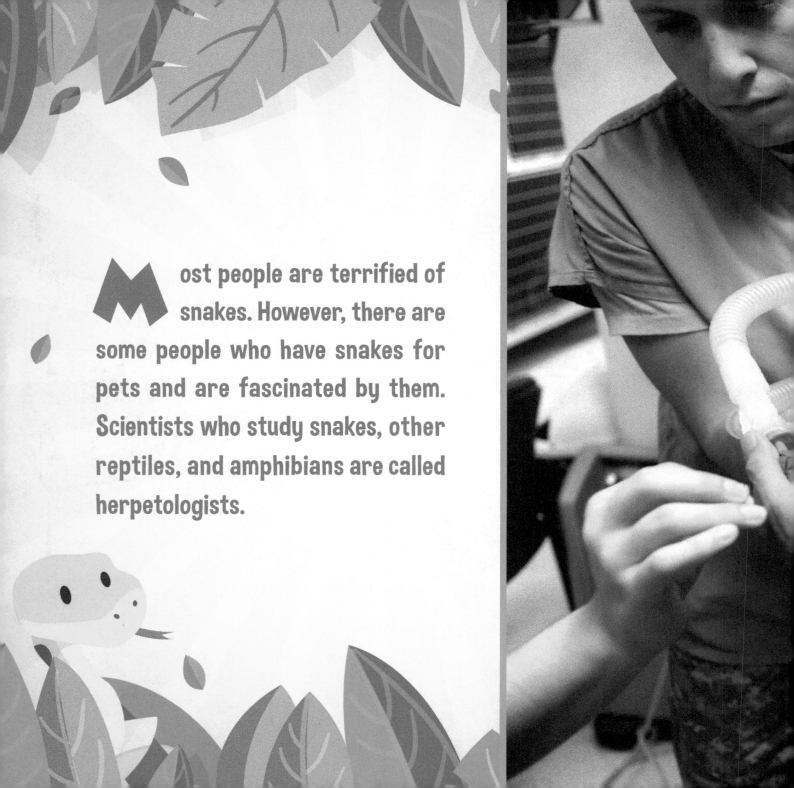

Most people are terrified of snakes. However, there are some people who have snakes for pets and are fascinated by them. Scientists who study snakes, other reptiles, and amphibians are called herpetologists.

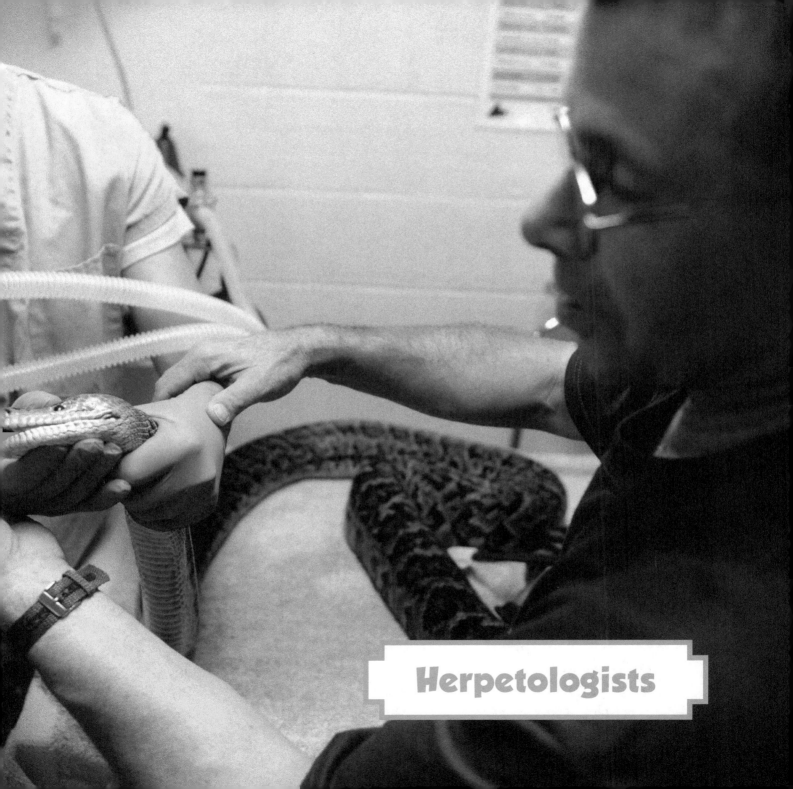

Herpetologists

HOW MANY SPECIES OF SNAKES ARE THERE?

There are over 3,000 different species of snakes worldwide. Most snakes are harmless to humans and will slide away when they come into contact with people. However, about 600 of the 3,000 species are venomous. Venomous snakes are very dangerous to humans and other animals. They bite with their fangs and then release a toxin into their victim's bloodstream, which can cause severe injury or death.

Venomous snakes are not the only snakes that are dangerous to humans. There are some snakes that squeeze their victims to death. These non-venomous snakes, such as pythons and anacondas, have been known to kill humans by biting them first, restricting their blood flow by squeezing them to death, and then swallowing them whole. Luckily, this is a very rare occurrence worldwide.

Green Anaconda

Cobra

WHY DO SNAKES HISS, SPIT, AND BITE?

Each different snake species has different ways to ward off attackers. Many snakes that are confronted will just turn and slide away as quickly as possible. Some snakes will raise their heads and hiss to scare off predators. Hissing is a scary, intimidating sound and it usually deters a snake's potential attacker by making the snake seem even more dangerous than it is.

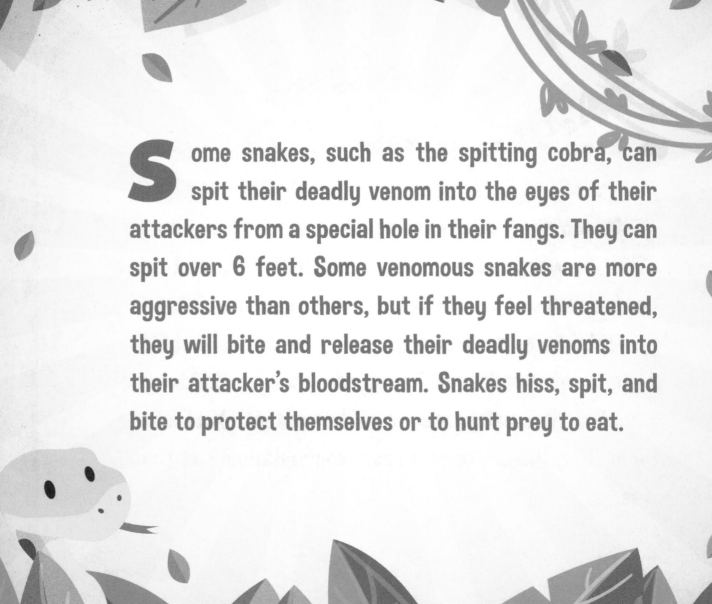

Some snakes, such as the spitting cobra, can spit their deadly venom into the eyes of their attackers from a special hole in their fangs. They can spit over 6 feet. Some venomous snakes are more aggressive than others, but if they feel threatened, they will bite and release their deadly venoms into their attacker's bloodstream. Snakes hiss, spit, and bite to protect themselves or to hunt prey to eat.

WHAT'S THE DIFFERENCE BETWEEN POISONOUS AND VENOMOUS?

Many people confuse the words "poisonous" and "venomous."

Tiger Snake

"Poisonous" means that an animal or plant is toxic to you if you consume it or touch it. "Venomous" describes an animal that injects a deadly toxin into prey to capture them for food or to ward off attacks. For example, a rattlesnake isn't poisonous because humans can actually eat rattlesnake meat. However, if you're bitten by a rattlesnake it will release venom into your body and that venom can kill you. There's only one snake species that's venomous as well as poisonous. It's the Asian Tiger snake, which has venom in its bite, but also collects poison in its skin that comes from its diet of toads.

WHERE DO VENOMOUS SNAKES LIVE?

Snakes that are venomous live all over the world. Antarctica is the only continent where there are no venomous snakes. They are most abundant in tropical areas.

Antartica

IN WHAT TYPES OF HABITATS ARE VENOMOUS SNAKES FOUND?

Over a long period of time, venomous snakes have adapted to live in many different types of habitats. Some have adapted to live in the desert with little water. Others live in humid, tropical environments, such as rainforests. They can thrive anywhere where there are warm temperatures for at least part of the year and abundant sources of food.

WHAT TYPE OF VENOM DO VENOMOUS SNAKES HAVE?

Venom is actually a toxic mix of various enzymes composed of different proteins. Every species that is venomous has venom that is unique to its species. The types of venoms can be categorized into three main categories.

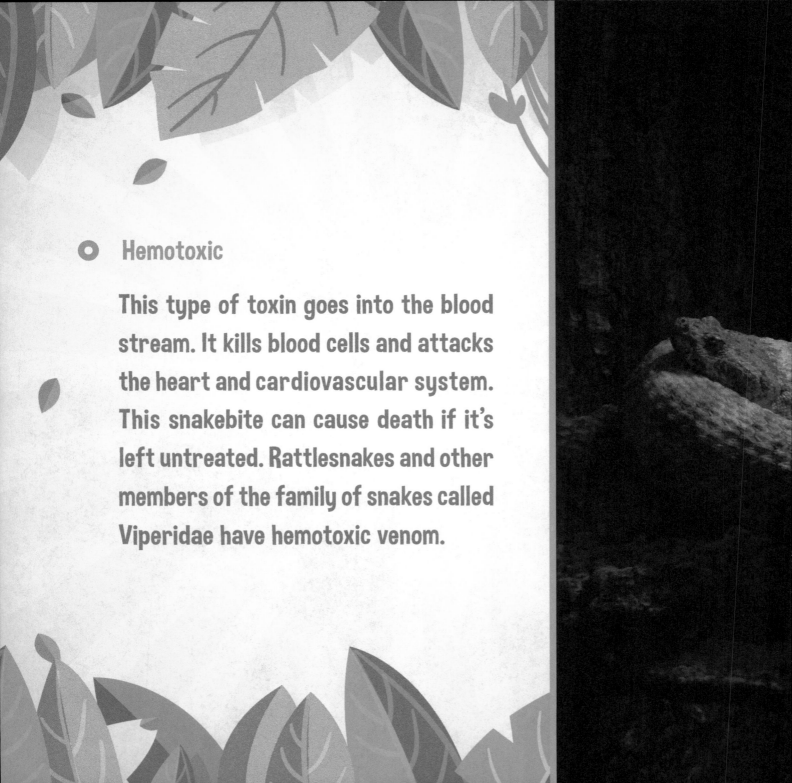

○ **Hemotoxic**

This type of toxin goes into the blood stream. It kills blood cells and attacks the heart and cardiovascular system. This snakebite can cause death if it's left untreated. Rattlesnakes and other members of the family of snakes called Viperidae have hemotoxic venom.

Rattlesnake

Green Mamba

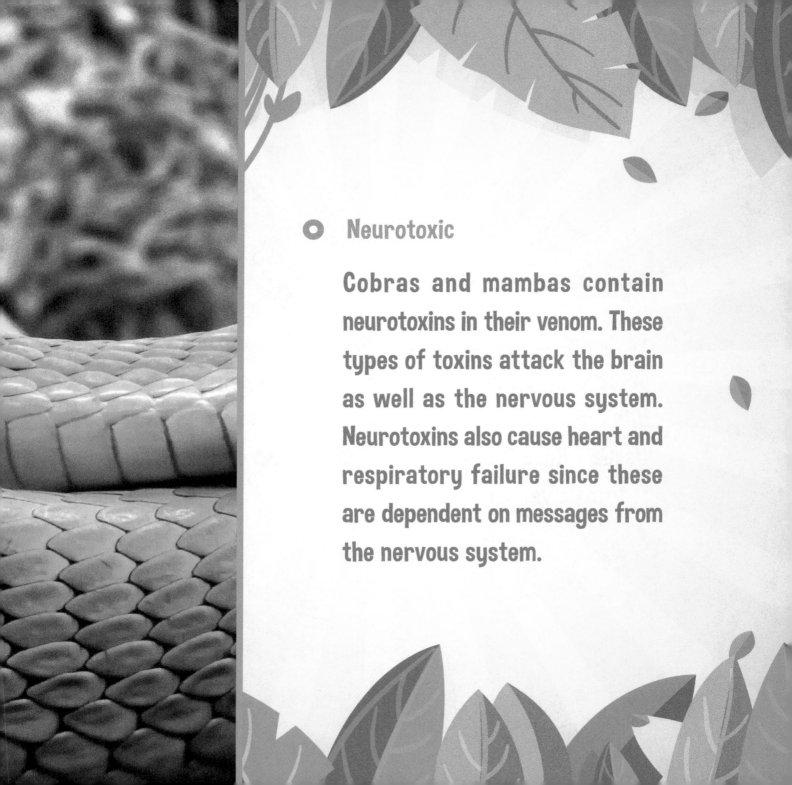

◯ Neurotoxic

Cobras and mambas contain neurotoxins in their venom. These types of toxins attack the brain as well as the nervous system. Neurotoxins also cause heart and respiratory failure since these are dependent on messages from the nervous system.

Cytotoxic

The word "cytotoxic" means "toxic to tissues composed of cells." Cytotoxic venom attacks the cells at the bite's location. It can cause the death of surrounding tissues. Russell's vipers and Lance Head vipers have cytotoxic venom.

Viper

There are other types of snake venom, but most of them fall into these three major categories. Some venomous snakes have combinations of all three types.

HOW DO VENOMOUS SNAKES HUNT FOR FOOD?

In addition to the different forms of venom, venomous snakes also have different hunting styles. There are two major ways they hunt.

Active Hunters

Some venomous snakes actively chase down their potential prey. The African boomslang snake hunts this way. It climbs up trees as it looks for birds, small animals, and chameleons to eat.

Ambush Hunters

Ambush hunter snakes are typically thicker and heavier than active hunters. Instead of chasing after their food, they wait until their prey gets close enough. Then, they spring up and bite their prey, injecting their toxic venom. Many of these snakes blend into their environment with skin colors and patterns that camouflage them. One example of an ambush hunter is the Gaboon viper.

HOW DO THEY INJECT THE VENOM?

There's a special gland inside the snake's head that creates the toxins for the venom. Then, there's a canal that connects this gland to the snake's fangs. When a venomous snake takes a bite into its prey, the venom flows quickly from the gland to the canal to the fangs, which are partially hollowed out for the venom to flow through. The venom travels from the fangs into the bite and spreads through the body of the snake's prey. This process happens in just a second or two.

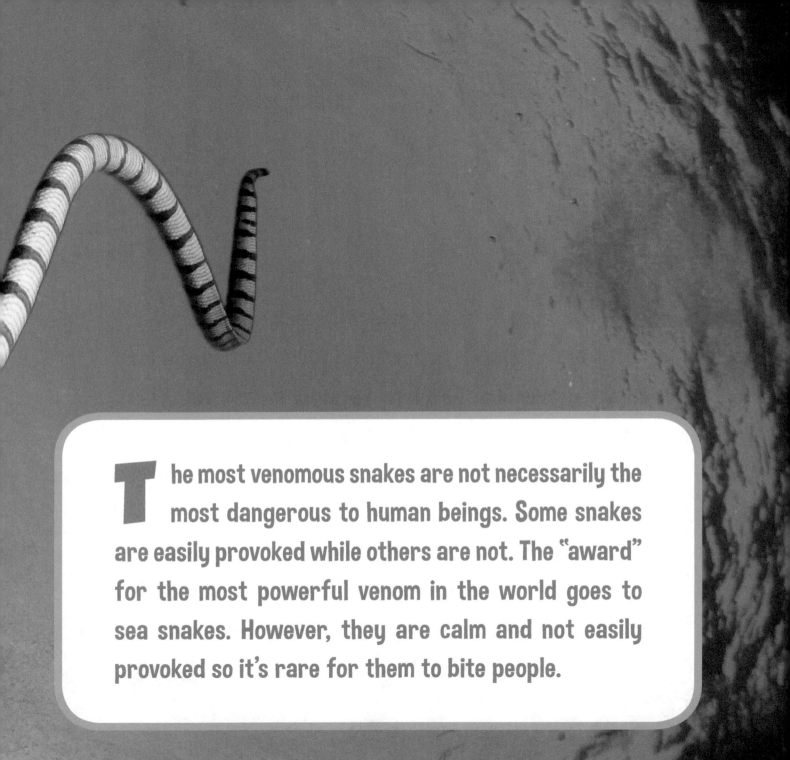

The most venomous snakes are not necessarily the most dangerous to human beings. Some snakes are easily provoked while others are not. The "award" for the most powerful venom in the world goes to sea snakes. However, they are calm and not easily provoked so it's rare for them to bite people.

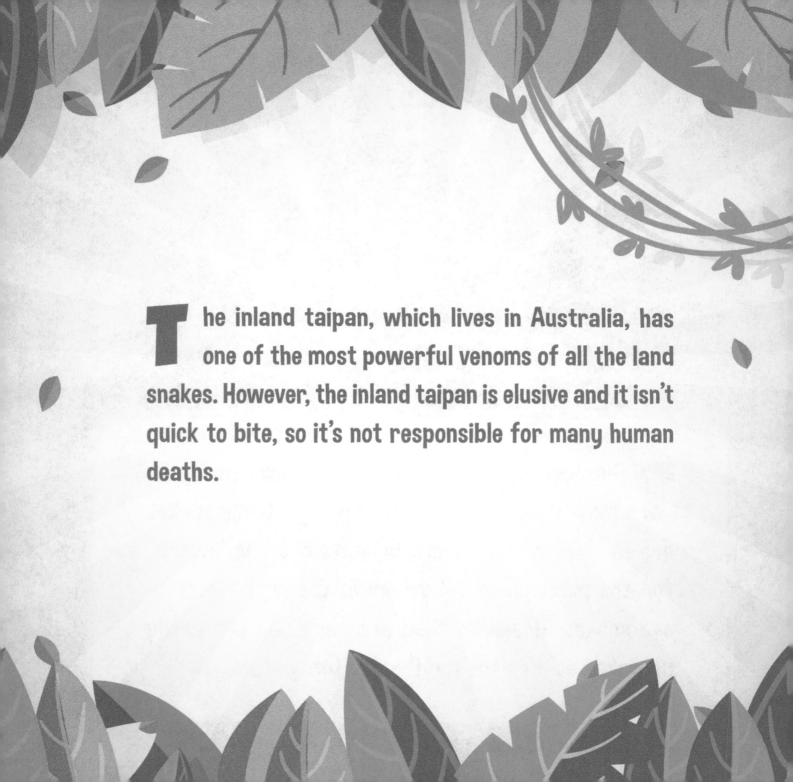

The inland taipan, which lives in Australia, has one of the most powerful venoms of all the land snakes. However, the inland taipan is elusive and it isn't quick to bite, so it's not responsible for many human deaths.

Inland Taipan

Sri Lanka

Some herpetologists believe that the most dangerous venomous snake is the Russell's viper, which lives in Sri Lanka. There are four reasons:

- It's often found close to places where people live.

- It possesses very deadly venom.

- It's quick to bite when it's the least bit provoked.

- It lives in a section of Asia that has agricultural expanses and paddies where rice is grown. There isn't much access to medical treatment if someone is bitten.

Due to these different combined factors, Russell's viper is responsible for more human deaths around the world than any other venomous snake.

Russell's Viper

WHICH VENOMOUS SNAKE IS THE LARGEST?

Although the eastern diamondback is considered to be the venomous snake that weighs the most, the king cobra attains the longest length. These massive snakes grow to 18-foot-lengths.

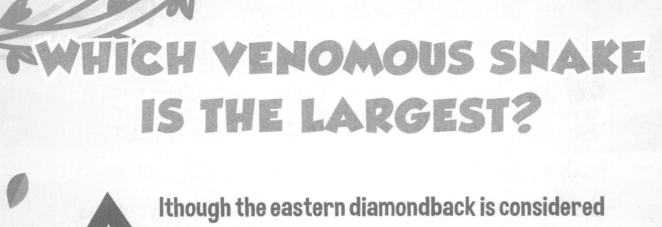

WHICH CONSTRICTOR SNAKE IS THE LARGEST?

The most dangerous of the non-venomous snakes are the constrictor snakes. The reticulated python, which lives in southeastern Asia as well as in the East Indies, grows to 30 feet in length and weighs 250 pounds or more. It's the longest snake in the world. The heaviest snake worldwide is the green anaconda. It's also a constrictor snake and can get as heavy as 550 pounds. These snakes pale by comparison to a fossil snake that was over 49 feet in length, longer than a school bus.

MYTHS ABOUT VENOMOUS SNAKES

There are many myths about snakes that bite and deliver venom. Here are three of these common myths.

VENOMOUS SNAKES ALWAYS HAVE HEADS THAT ARE SHAPED LIKE TRIANGLES.

This is a myth. Some venomous snakes do have triangular heads from their venom glands, but there are many that don't have heads shaped this way. The coral snake is an example of a venomous snake that doesn't have a triangular head.

Coral Snake

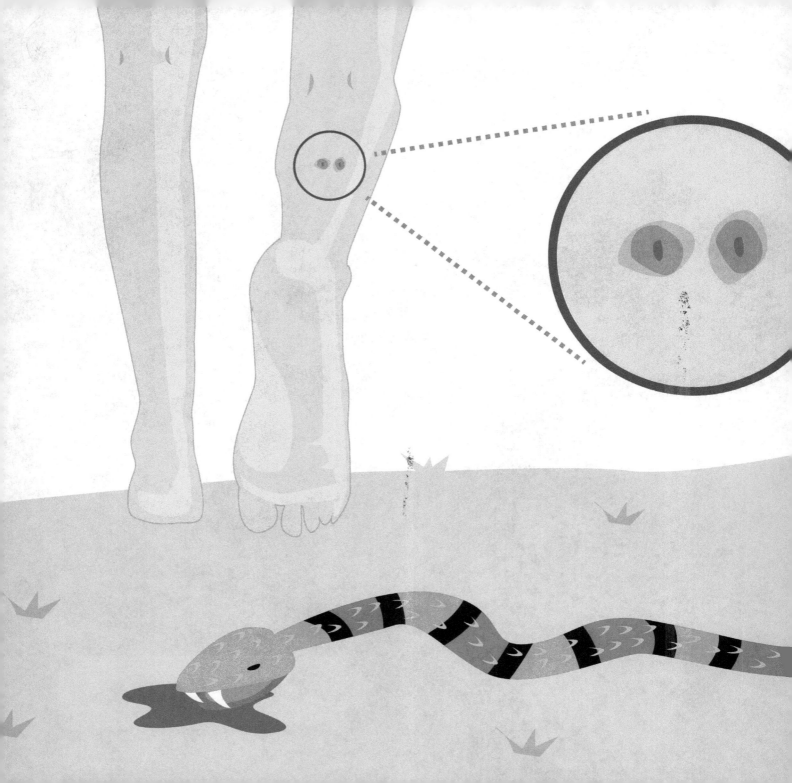

IF YOU GET BITTEN BY A SNAKE, YOU SHOULD SUCK OUT THE VENOM.

This is a dangerous myth that could cost you your life. Suction won't get the venom out of your body. The only way to treat a snakebite that's venomous is to get an antivenom.

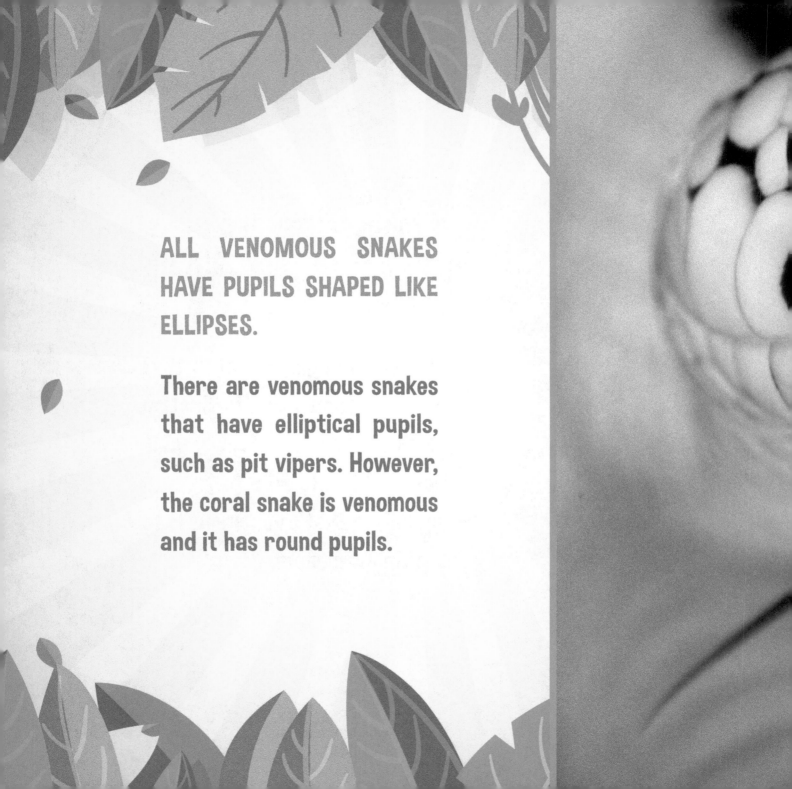

ALL VENOMOUS SNAKES HAVE PUPILS SHAPED LIKE ELLIPSES.

There are venomous snakes that have elliptical pupils, such as pit vipers. However, the coral snake is venomous and it has round pupils.

Desert Snake

SUMMARY

Deadly snakes are venomous, not poisonous. They hiss, spit, and bite to ward off attackers and to capture prey to eat. Their venom is formed in a gland in their heads and travels into a canal and into their fangs. When they bite another animal, their venom quickly flows into the blood or tissues of their prey. Venomous snakes aren't the only snakes that are dangerous to humans. Non-venomous constrictor snakes are very dangerous too.

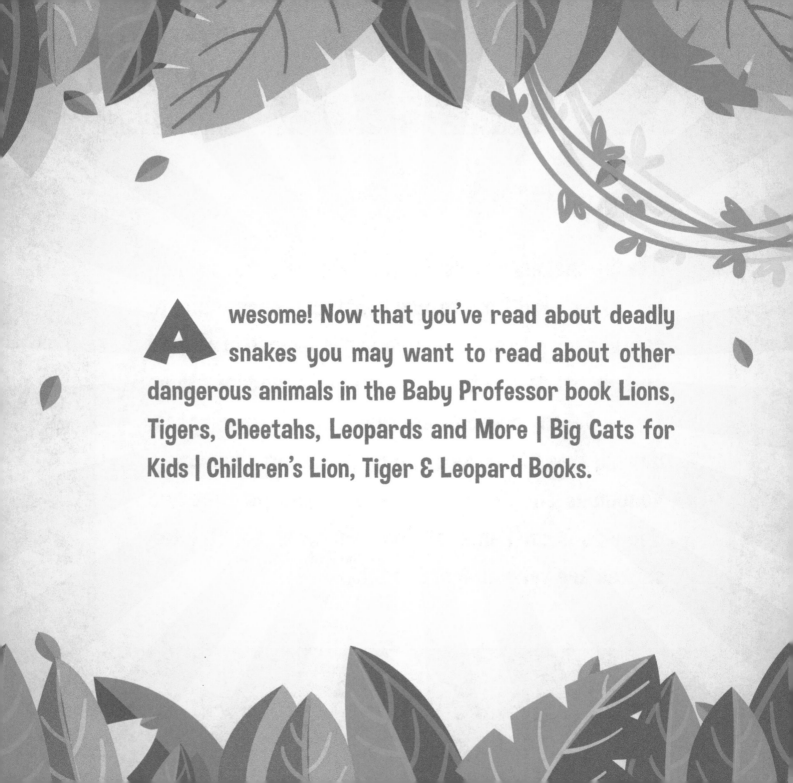

Awesome! Now that you've read about deadly snakes you may want to read about other dangerous animals in the Baby Professor book Lions, Tigers, Cheetahs, Leopards and More | Big Cats for Kids | Children's Lion, Tiger & Leopard Books.